BETHINK YOURSELVES!

LEO TOLSTOY

TRUE SIGN
PUBLISHING HOUSE

Published by True Sign Publishing House
Address: SY. No. 21/2 & 21/3, Sonnenahalli,
Krishnarajapural, Bengaluru,
Karnataka - 560049 India
E-mail: truesignbooks@gmail.com
Website: www.truesign.in

Bethink Yourselves!
Author: Leo Tolstoy

ISBN: 978-93-5462-974-7

First Edition: 2022

Contents

I 5
II 8
III 11
IV 14
V 17
VI 20
VII 23
VIII 25
IX 28
X 31
XI 34
XII 39

"This is your hour, and the power of darkness."

—LUKE xxii. 53.

I

AGAIN war. Again sufferings, necessary to nobody, utterly uncalled for; again fraud; again the universal stupefaction and brutalization of men.

Men who are separated from each other by thousands of miles, hundreds of thousands of such men (on the one hand—Buddhists, whose law forbids the killing, not only of men, but of animals; on the other hand—Christians, professing the law of brotherhood and love) like wild beasts on land and on sea are seeking out each other, in order to kill, torture, and mutilate each other in the most cruel way. What can this be? Is it a dream or a reality? Something is taking place which should not, cannot be; one longs to believe that it is a dream and to awake from it. But no, it is not a dream, it is a dreadful reality!

One could yet understand how a poor, uneducated, defrauded Japanese, torn from his field and taught that Buddhism consists not in compassion to all that lives, but in sacrifices to idols, and how a similar poor illiterate fellow from the neighborhood of Toula or Nijni Novgorod, who has been taught that Christianity consists in worshipping Christ, the Madonna, Saints, and their ikons—one could understand how these unfortunate men, brought by the violence and deceit of centuries to recognize the greatest crime in the world—the murder of one's brethren—as a virtuous act, can commit these dreadful deeds, without regarding themselves as being guilty in so doing.

But how can so-called enlightened men preach war, support it, participate in it, and, worst of all, without suffering the dangers of war themselves, incite others to it, sending their unfortunate defrauded brothers to fight? These so-called enlightened men cannot possibly ignore, I do not say the Christian law, if they recognize themselves to be Christians, but all that has been written, is being written, has and is being said, about the cruelty, futility, and senselessness of war. They are regarded as enlightened men precisely because they know all this. The majority of them have themselves written and spoken about this. Not to mention The Hague Conference, which called forth universal praise, or all the books, pamphlets, newspaper articles, and speeches demonstrating the possibility of the solution of international misunderstandings by international arbitration—no enlightened man can help knowing that the universal competition in the armaments of States must inevitably lead them to endless wars, or to a general bankruptcy, or to both the one and the other. They cannot but know that besides the senseless, purposeless expenditure of milliards of roubles, *i.e.* of human labor, on the preparations for war, during the wars themselves millions of the most energetic and vigorous men perish in that period of their life which is best for productive labor (during the past century wars have destroyed fourteen million men). Enlightened men cannot but know that occasions for war are always such as are not worth not only one human life, but not one hundredth part of all that which is spent upon wars (in fighting for the emancipation of the negroes much more was spent than it would have cost to redeem them from slavery).

Every one knows and cannot help knowing that, above all, wars, calling forth the lowest animal passions, deprave and brutalize men. Every one knows the weakness of the arguments in favor of war, such as were brought forward by De Maistre, Moltke, and others, for they are all founded on the sophism that in every human calamity it is possible to find an advantageous element, or else upon the utterly arbitrary assertion that wars have always existed and therefore always must exist, as if the bad actions of men could be justified by the advantages or the usefulness which they realize, or by the consideration that they have been committed during a long period of time. All so-called enlightened men know all this.

Then suddenly war begins, and all this is instantly forgotten, and the same men who but yesterday were proving the cruelty, futility, the senselessness of wars now think, speak, and write only about killing as many men as possible, about ruining and destroying the greatest possible amount of the productions of human labor, and about exciting as much as possible the passion of hatred in those peaceful, harmless, industrious men who by their labor feed, clothe, maintain these same pseudo-enlightened men, who compel them to commit those dreadful deeds contrary to their conscience, welfare, or faith.

II

SOMETHING is taking place incomprehensible and impossible in its cruelty, falsehood, and stupidity. The Russian Tsar, the same man who exhorted all the nations in the cause of peace, publicly announces that, notwithstanding all his efforts to maintain the peace so dear to his heart (efforts which express themselves in the seizing of other peoples' lands and in the strengthening of armies for the defence of these stolen lands), he, owing to the attack of the Japanese, commands that the same shall be done to the Japanese as they had commenced doing to the Russians—*i.e.* that they should be slaughtered; and in announcing this call to murder he mentions God, asking the Divine blessing on the most dreadful crime in the world. The Japanese Emperor has proclaimed the same thing in relation to the Russians.

Men of science and of law (Messieurs Muravieff and Martens) strenuously try to prove that in the recent call of all nations to universal peace and the present incitement to war, because of the seizure of other peoples' lands, there is no contradiction. Diplomatists, in their refined French language, publish and send out circulars in which they circumstantially and diligently prove (though they know no one believes them) that, after all its efforts to establish peaceful relations (in reality, after all its efforts to deceive other countries), the Russian Government has been compelled to have recourse to the only means for a rational solution of the question—*i.e.* to the murder of men. The same thing is written by Japanese diplomatists. Scientists, historians, and philosophers, on their side, comparing the present with the past, deduce from these comparisons profound conclusions, and argue interminably about the laws of the movement of nations, about the relation between the yellow and white races, or about Buddhism and Christianity, and on the basis of these deductions and arguments justify the slaughter of those belonging to the yellow race by Christians; while in the same way the Japanese scientists and philosophers justify the slaughter of those of the white race. Journalists, without concealing their joy, try to outdo each other, and, not hesitating at any falsehood, however impudent and transparent, prove in all possible ways that the Russians only are right and strong and good in every respect, and that all the Japanese are wrong and weak and bad in every respect, and that all those are also bad who are inimical or may become inimical toward the Russians—the English, the Americans; and the same is proved likewise by the Japanese and their supporters in relation to the Russians.

Not to mention the military, who in the way of their profession prepare for murder, crowds of so-called enlightened people, such as professors, social reformers, students, nobles, merchants, without being forced thereto by anything or anybody, express the most bitter and contemptuous feelings toward the Japanese, the English, or the Americans, toward whom but yesterday they were either well-disposed or indifferent; while, without the least compulsion, they express the most abject, servile feelings toward the Tsar (to whom, to say the least, they were completely indifferent), assuring him of their unlimited love and readiness to sacrifice their lives in his interests.

This unfortunate, entangled young man, recognized as the leader of one hundred and thirty millions of people, continually deceived and compelled to contradict himself, confidently thanks and blesses the troops whom he calls his own for murder in defence of lands which with yet less right he also calls his own. All present to each other hideous ikons in which not only no one amongst the educated believes, but which unlearned peasants are beginning to abandon; all bow down to the ground before these ikons, kiss them, and pronounce pompous and deceitful speeches in which no one really believes.

Wealthy people contribute insignificant portions of their immorally acquired riches for this cause of murder or the organization of help in connection with the work of murder; while the poor, from whom the Government annually collects two milliards, deem it necessary to do likewise, giving their mites also. The Government incites and encourages crowds of idlers, who walk about the streets with the Tsar's portrait, singing, shouting hurrah! and who, under pretext of patriotism, are licensed in all kinds of excess. All over Russia, from the Palace to the remotest village, the pastors of churches, calling themselves Christians, appeal to that God who has enjoined love to one's enemies—to the God of Love Himself—to help the work of the devil to further the slaughter of men.

Stupefied by prayers, sermons, exhortations, by processions, pictures, and newspapers, the cannon's flesh, hundreds of thousands of men, uniformly dressed, carrying divers deadly weapons, leaving their parents, wives, children, with hearts of agony, but with artificial sprightliness, go where they, risking their own lives, will commit the most dreadful act of killing men whom they do not know and who have done them no harm. And they are followed by doctors and nurses, who somehow imagine that at home they cannot serve simple, peaceful, suffering people, but can only serve those who are engaged in slaughtering each other. Those who remain at home are gladdened by news of the murder of men, and when they learn that many Japanese have been killed they thank some one whom they call God.

All this is not only regarded as the manifestation of elevated feeling, but those who refrain from such manifestations, if they endeavor to disabuse men, are deemed traitors and betrayers, and are in danger of being abused and beaten by a brutalized crowd which, in defence of its insanity and cruelty, can possess no other weapon than brute force.

III

IT is as if there had never existed either Voltaire, or Montaigne, or Pascal, or Swift, or Kant, or Spinoza, or hundreds of other writers who have exposed, with great force, the madness and futility of war, and have described its cruelty, immorality, and savagery; and, above all, it is as if there had never existed Jesus and his teaching of human brotherhood and love of God and of men.

One recalls all this to mind and looks around on what is now taking place, and one experiences horror less at the abominations of war than at that which is the most horrible of all horrors—the consciousness of the impotency of human reason. That which alone distinguishes man from the animal, that which constitutes his merit—his reason—is found to be an unnecessary, and not only a useless, but a pernicious addition, which simply impedes action, like a bridle fallen from a horse's head, and entangled in his legs and only irritating him.

It is comprehensible that a heathen, a Greek, a Roman, even a mediæval Christian, ignorant of the Gospel and blindly believing all the prescriptions of the Church, might fight and, fighting, pride himself on his military achievements; but how can a believing Christian, or even a sceptic, involuntarily permeated by the Christian ideals of human brotherhood and love which have inspired the works of the philosophers, moralists, and artists of our time,—how can such take a gun, or stand by a cannon, and aim at a crowd of his fellow-men, desiring to kill as many of them as possible?

The Assyrians, Romans, or Greeks might be persuaded that in fighting they were acting not only according to their conscience, but even fulfilling a righteous deed. But, whether we wish it or not, we are Christians, and however Christianity may have been distorted, its general spirit cannot but lift us to that higher plane of reason whence we can no longer refrain from feeling with our whole being not only the senselessness and the cruelty of war, but its complete opposition to all that we regard as good and right. Therefore, we cannot do as they did, with assurance, firmness, and peace, and without a consciousness of our criminality, without the desperate feeling of a murderer, who, having begun to kill his victim, and feeling in the depths of his soul the guilt of his act, proceeds to try to stupefy or infuriate himself, to be able the better to complete his dreadful deed. All the unnatural, feverish, hot-headed, insane excitement which has now seized the idle upper ranks of Russian society is merely the symptom of their recognition of the criminality of the work which is being done. All these insolent, mendacious speeches about devotion to, and worship of, the Monarch, about readiness to sacrifice life (or one should say other people's lives, and not one's own); all these promises to defend with one's breast land which does not belong to one; all these senseless benedictions of each other with various banners and monstrous ikons; all these *Te Deums*; all these preparations of blankets and bandages; all these detachments of nurses; all these contributions to the fleet and to the Red Cross presented to the Government, whose direct duty is (whilst it has the possibility of collecting from the people as much money as it requires), having declared war, to organize the necessary fleet and necessary means for attending the wounded; all these Slavonic, pompous, senseless, and blasphemous prayers, the utterance of which in various towns is communicated in the papers as important news; all these processions, calls for the national hymn, cheers; all this dreadful, desperate newspaper mendacity, which, being universal, does not fear exposure; all this stupefaction and brutalization which has now taken hold of Russian society, and which is being transmitted by degrees also to the masses; all this is only a symptom of the guilty consciousness of that dreadful act which is being accomplished.

Spontaneous feeling tells men that what they are doing should not be; but, as the murderer who has begun to assassinate his victim cannot stop, so also Russian people now imagine that the fact of the deadly work having been commenced is an unanswerable argument in favor of war. War has been begun, and therefore it should go on. Thus it seems to simple, benighted, unlearned men, acting under the influence of the petty passions and stupefaction to which they have been subjected. In exactly the same way the most educated men of our time argue to prove that man does not possess free will, and that, therefore, even were he to understand that the work he has commenced is evil, he can no longer cease to do it. And dazed, brutalized men continue their dreadful work.

IV

ASK a soldier, a private, a corporal, a non-commissioned officer, who has abandoned his old parents, his wife, his children, why he is preparing to kill men whom he does not know; he will at first be astonished at your question. He is a soldier, he has taken the oath, and it is his duty to fulfil the orders of his commanders. If you tell him that war—*i.e.* the slaughter of men—does not conform to the command, "Thou shalt not kill," he will say: "And how if ours are attacked—For the King—For the Orthodox faith?" (One of them said in answer to my question: "And how if he attacks that which is sacred?" "What do you mean?" I asked. "Why," said he, "the banner.") And if you endeavor to explain to such a soldier that God's Commandment is more important not only than the banner but than anything else in the world, he will become silent, or he will get angry and report you to the authorities.

Ask an officer, a general, why he goes to the war. He will tell you that he is a military man, and that the military are indispensable for the defence of the fatherland. As to murder not conforming to the spirit of the Christian law, this does not trouble him, as either he does not believe in this law, or, if he does, it is not in the law itself, but in that explanation which has been given to this law. But, above all, he, like the soldier, in place of the personal question, what should he do himself, always put the general question about the State, or the fatherland. "At the present moment, when the fatherland is in danger, one should act, and not argue," he will say.

Ask the diplomatists, who, by their deceits, prepare wars, why they do it. They will tell you that the object of their activity is the establishment of peace between nations, and that this object is attained, not by ideal, unrealizable theories, but by diplomatic action and readiness for war. And, just as the military, instead of the question concerning one's own action, place the general question, so also diplomatists will speak about the interests of Russia, about the unscrupulousness of other Powers, about the balance of power in Europe, but not about their own position and its activities.

Ask the journalists why, by their writings, they incite men to war; they will say that wars in general are necessary and useful, especially the present war, and they will confirm this opinion of theirs by misty patriotic phrases, and, just like the military and diplomatist, to the question why he, a journalist, a particular individual, a living man, acts in a certain way, he will speak about the general interests of the nation, about the State, civilization, the white race. In the same way, all those who prepare war will explain their participation in that work. They will perhaps agree that it would be desirable to abolish war, but at present this is impossible. At present they as Russians and as men who occupy certain positions, such as heads of the nobility, representatives of local self-government, doctors, workers of the Red Cross, are called upon to act and not to argue. "There is no time to argue and to think of oneself," they will say, "when there is a great common work to be done." The same will be said by the Tsar, seemingly responsible for the whole thing. He, like the soldier, will be astonished at the question, whether war is now necessary. He does not even admit the idea that the war might yet be arrested. He will say that he cannot refrain from fulfilling that which is demanded of him by the whole nation, that, although he does recognize that war is a great evil, and has used, and is ready to use, all possible means for its abolition—in the present case he could not help declaring war, and cannot help continuing it. It is necessary for the welfare and glory of Russia.

Every one of these men, to the question why he, so and so, Ivan, Peter, Nicholas, whilst recognizing as binding upon him the Christian law which not only forbids the killing of one's neighbor but demands that one should love him, serve him, why he permits himself to participate in war; *i.e.* in violence, loot, murder, will infallibly answer the same thing, that he is thus acting in the name of his fatherland, or faith, or oath, or honor, or civilization, or the future welfare of the whole of mankind—in general, of something abstract and indefinite. Moreover, these men are always so urgently occupied either by preparation for war, or by its organization, or discussions about it, that in their leisure time they can only rest from their labors, and have not time to occupy themselves with discussions about their life, regarding such discussions as idle.

V

MEN of our Christian world and of our time are like a man who, having missed the right turning, the further he goes the more he becomes convinced that he is going the wrong way. Yet the greater his doubts, the quicker and the more desperately does he hurry on, consoling himself with the thought that he will arrive somewhere. But the time comes when it becomes quite clear that the way along which he is going will lead to nothing but a precipice, which he is already beginning to discern before him.

In such a position stands the Christian humanity of our time. It is perfectly evident that, if we continue to live as we are now living, guided in our private lives, as well as in the life of separate States, by the sole desire of welfare for ourselves and for our State, and will, as we do now, think to ensure this welfare by violence, then, inevitably increasing the means of violence of one against the other and of State against State, we shall, first, keep subjecting ourselves more and more, transferring the major portion of our productiveness to armaments; and, secondly, by killing in mutual wars the best physically developed men, we must become more and more degenerate and morally depraved.

That this will be the case if we do not alter our life is as certain as it is mathematically certain that two non-parallel straight lines must meet. But not only is this theoretically certain in our time; it is becoming certain not only to thought, but also to the consciousness. The precipice which we approach is already becoming apparent to us, and the most simple, non-philosophizing, and uneducated men cannot but see that, by arming ourselves more and more against each other and slaughtering each other in war, we, like spiders in a jar, can come to nothing else but the destruction of each other.

A sincere, serious, rational man can no longer console himself by the thought that matters can be mended, as was formerly supposed, by a universal empire such as that of Rome or of Charles the Great, or Napoleon, or by the mediæval spiritual power of the Pope, or by Holy Alliances, by the political balance of the European Concert, and by peaceful international tribunals, or, as some have thought, by the increase of military strength and the newly discovered powerful weapons of destruction.

It is impossible to organize a universal empire or republic, consisting of European States, as different nationalities will never desire to unite into one State. To organize international tribunals for the solution of international disputes? But who will impose obedience to the decision of the tribunal upon a contending party who has an organized army of millions of men? To disarm? No one desires it or will begin it. To invent yet more dreadful means of destruction—balloons with bombs filled with suffocating gases, shells, which men will shower upon each other from above? Whatever may be invented, all States will furnish themselves with similar weapons of destruction. And cannon's flesh, as after cold weapons it submitted to bullets, and meekly exposed itself to shells, bombs, far-reaching guns, mitrailleuses, mines, so it will also submit to bombs charged with suffocating gases scattered down upon it from balloons.

Nothing shows more evidently than the speeches of M. Muravieff and Professor Martens about the Japanese war not contradicting The Hague Peace Conference—nothing shows more obviously than these speeches to what an extent, amongst the men of our time, the means for the transmission of thought—speech—is distorted, and how the capacity for clear, rational thinking is completely lost. Thought and speech are used for the purpose, not of serving as a guide for human activity, but of justifying any activity, however criminal it may be. The late Boer war and the present Japanese war, which can at any moment pass into a universal slaughter, have proved this beyond all doubt. All anti-military discussions can as little contribute to the cessation of war as the most eloquent and persuasive considerations addressed to fighting dogs as to its being more advantageous to divide the piece of meat over which they are struggling than to mutilate each other and lose the piece of meat, which will be carried away by some passing dog not joining in the fight. We are dashing on toward the precipice, cannot stop, and we are approaching its edge.

For every rational man who reflects upon the position in which humanity is now placed and upon that which it is inevitably approaching, it cannot but be obvious that there is no practical issue out of this position, that one cannot devise any combination or organization which would save us from the destruction toward which we are inevitably rushing. Not to mention the economical problems which become more and more complex, those mutual relations between the States arming themselves against each other and at any moment ready to break out into wars clearly point to the certain destruction toward which all so-called civilized humanity is being carried. Then what is to be done?

VI

Two thousand years ago John the Baptist and then Jesus said to men: The time is fulfilled and the Kingdom of God is at hand; (μετανοεῖτε) bethink yourselves and believe in the Gospel (Mark i. 15); and if you do not bethink yourselves you will all perish (Luke xiii. 5).

But men did not listen to them, and the destruction they foretold is already near at hand. And we men of our time cannot but see it. We are already perishing, and, therefore, we cannot leave unheeded that—old in time, but for us new—means of salvation. We cannot but see that, besides all the other calamities which flow from our bad and irrational life, military preparations alone and the wars inevitably growing from them must infallibly destroy us. We cannot but see that all the means of escape invented by men from these evils are found and must be found to be ineffectual, and that the disastrous position of the nations arming themselves against each other cannot but go on advancing continually. And therefore the words of Jesus refer to us and our time more than to any time or to any one.

Jesus said, "Bethink yourselves"—*i.e.* "Let every man interrupt the work he has begun and ask himself: Who am I? From whence have I appeared, and in what consists my destiny? And having answered these questions, according to the answer decide whether that which thou doest is in conformity with thy destiny." And every man of our world and time, that is, being acquainted with the essence of the Christian teaching, needs only for a minute to interrupt his activity, to forget the capacity in which he is regarded by men, be it of Emperor, soldier, minister, or journalist, and seriously ask himself who he is and what is his destiny—in order to begin to doubt the utility, lawfulness, and reasonableness of his actions. "Before I am Emperor, soldier, minister, or journalist," must say to himself every man of our time and of the Christian world, "before any of these, I am a man—*i.e.* an organic being sent by the Higher Will into a universe infinite in time and space, in order, after staying in it for an instant, to die—*i.e.* to disappear from it. And, therefore, all those personal, social, and even universal human aims which I may place before myself and which are placed before me by men are all insignificant, owing to the shortness of my life as well as to the infiniteness of the life of the universe, and should be subordinated to that higher aim for the attainment of which I am sent into the world. This ultimate aim, owing to my limitations, is inaccessible to me, but it does exist (as there must be a purpose in all that exists), and my business is that of being its instrument—*i.e.* my destiny, my vocation, is that of being a workman of God, of fulfilling His work." And having understood this destiny, every man of our world and time, from Emperor to soldier, cannot but regard differently those duties which he has taken upon himself or other men have imposed upon him.

"Before I was crowned, recognized as Emperor," must the Emperor say to himself: "before I undertook to fulfil the duties of the head of the State, I, by the very fact that I live, have promised to fulfil that which is demanded of me by the Higher Will that sent me into life. These demands I not only know, but feel in my heart. They consist, as it is expressed in the Christian law, which I profess, in that I should submit to the will of God, and fulfil that which it requires of me, that I should love my neighbor, serve him, and act towards him as I would wish others to act towards me. Am I doing this?—ruling men, prescribing violence, executions, and, the most dreadful of all,—wars. Men tell me that I ought to do this. But God says that I ought to do something quite different. And, therefore, however much I may be told that, as the head of the State, I must direct acts of violence, the levying of taxes, executions and, above all, war, that is, the slaughter of one's neighbor, I do not wish to and cannot do these things."

So must say to himself the soldier, who is taught that he must kill men, and the minister, who deemed it his duty to prepare for war, and the journalist who incited to war, and every man, who puts to himself the question, Who is he, what is his destination in life? And the moment the head of the State will cease to direct war, the soldier to fight, the minister to prepare means for war, the journalist to incite thereto—then, without any new institutions, adaptations, balance of power, tribunals, there will of itself be destroyed that hopeless position in which men have placed themselves, not only in relation to war, but also to all other calamities which they themselves inflict upon themselves.

So that, however strange this may appear, the most effective and certain deliverance of men from all the calamities which they inflict upon themselves and from the most dreadful of all—war—is attainable, not by any external general measures, but merely by that simple appeal to the consciousness of each separate man which, nineteen hundred years ago, was proposed by Jesus—that every man bethink himself, and ask himself, who is he, why he lives, and what he should and should not do.

VII

The evil from which men of our time are suffering is produced by the fact that the majority live without that which alone affords a rational guidance for human activity—without religion; not that religion which consists in belief in dogmas, in the fulfilment of rites which afford a pleasant diversion, consolation, stimulant, but that religion which establishes the relation of man to the All, to God, and, therefore, gives a general higher direction to all human activity, and without which people stand on the plane of animals and even lower than they. This evil which is leading men to inevitable destruction has manifested itself with special power in our time, because, having lost all rational guidance in life, and having directed all efforts to discoveries and improvements principally in the sphere of technical knowledge, men of our time have developed in themselves enormous power over the forces of nature; but, not having any guidance for the rational adaptation of this power, they naturally have used it for the satisfaction of their lowest and most animal propensities.

Bereft of religion, men possessing enormous power over the forces of nature are like children to whom powder or explosive gas has been given as a plaything. Considering this power which men of our time possess, and the way they use it, one feels that considering the degree of their moral development men have no right, not only to the use of railways, steam, electricity, telephones, photography, wireless telegraphs, but even to the simple art of manufacturing iron and steel, as all these improvements and arts they use only for the satisfaction of their lusts, for amusement, dissipation, and the destruction of each other.

Then, what is to be done? To reject all these improvements of life, all this power acquired by humanity—to forget that which it has learnt? This is impossible, however perniciously these mental acquisitions are used; they still are acquisitions, and men cannot forget them. To alter those combinations of nations which have been formed during centuries and to establish new ones? To invent such new institutions as would hinder the minority from deceiving and exploiting the majority? To disseminate knowledge? All this has been tried, and is being done with great fervor. All these imaginary methods of improvement represent the chief methods of self-oblivion and of diverting one's attention from the consciousness of inevitable perdition. The boundaries of States are changed, institutions are altered, knowledge is disseminated; but within other boundaries, with other organizations, with increased knowledge, men remain the same beasts, ready any minute to tear each other to pieces, or the same slaves they have always been, and always will be, while they continue to be guided, not by religious consciousness, but by passions, theories, and external influences.

Man has no choice; he must be the slave of the most unscrupulous and insolent amongst slaves, or else the servant of God, because for man there is only one way of being free—by uniting his will with the will of God. People bereft of religion, some repudiating religion itself, others recognizing as religion those external, monstrous forms which have superseded it, and guided only by their personal lusts, fear, human laws, and, above all, by mutual hypnotism, cannot cease to be animals or slaves, and no external efforts can extricate them from this state; for only religion makes a man free. And most of the people of our time are deprived of it.

VIII

"But, in order to abolish the evil from which we are suffering," those will say who are preoccupied by various practical activities, "it would be necessary that not a few men only, but all men, should bethink themselves, and that, having done so, they should uniformly understand the destination of their lives, in the fulfilment of the will of God and in the service of one's neighbor.

"Is this possible?" Not only possible, do I answer, but it is impossible that this should not take place. It is impossible for men not to bethink themselves—*i.e.* impossible that each man should not put to himself the question as to who he is and wherefore he lives; for man, as a rational being, cannot live without seeking to know why he lives, and he has always put to himself this question, and always, according to the degree of his development, has answered it in his religious teaching. In our time, the inner contradiction in which men feel themselves elicits this question with special insistence, and demands an answer. It is impossible for men of our time to answer this question otherwise than by recognizing the law of life in love to men and in the service of them, this being for our time the only rational answer as to the meaning of human life; and this answer nineteen hundred years ago has been expressed in the Christian religion and is likewise known to the vast majority of all mankind.

This answer in a latent state lives in the consciousness of all men of the Christian world of our time; but it does not openly express itself and serve as guidance for our life, only because, on the one hand, those who enjoy the greatest authority, so-called scientists, being under the coarse error that religion is a temporary and outgrown step in the development of mankind and that men can live without religion, inculcate this error to those of the masses who are beginning to be educated; and, on the other hand, because those in power, sometimes consciously, but often unconsciously (being under the error that the Church faith is Christian religion), endeavor to support and excite in the people crude superstitions given out as the Christian religion. If only these two deceptions were to be destroyed, then true religion, already latent in men of our time, would become evident and obligatory.

To bring this about it is necessary that, on the one hand, men of science should understand that the principle of the brotherhood of all men and the rule of not doing unto others what one does not wish for oneself is not one casual idea out of a multitude of human theories which can be subordinated to any other considerations, but is an incontestable principle, standing higher than the rest, and flowing from the changeless relation of man to that which is eternal, to God, and is religion, all religion, and, therefore, always obligatory.

On the other hand, it is necessary that those who consciously or unconsciously preach crude superstitions under the guise of Christianity should understand that all these dogmas, sacraments, and rites which they support and preach are not only, as they think, harmless, but are in the highest degree pernicious, concealing from men that central religious truth which is expressed in the fulfilment of God's will, in the service of men, and that the rule of acting toward others as one would wish others to act toward oneself is not merely one of the prescriptions of the Christian religion, but is the whole of practical religion, as indeed is stated in the Gospels.

To bring about that men of our time should uniformly place before themselves the question of the meaning of life, and uniformly answer it, it is only necessary that those who regard themselves as enlightened should cease to think and to inculcate to other generations that religion is atavism, the survival of a past wild state, and that for the good life of men the spreading of education is sufficient—*i.e.* the spread of the most varied knowledge which is in some way to bring men to justice and to a moral life. These men should understand instead that for the good life of humanity religion is vital, and that this religion already exists and lives in the consciousness of the men of our time. Men who are intentionally and unintentionally stupefying the people by church superstitions should cease to do so, and recognize that what is important and binding in Christianity is not baptism, nor Communion, nor profession of dogmas, etc., but only love to God and to one's neighbor, and the fulfilling of the commandment of acting toward others as one wishes others to act toward oneself—and that in this lies all the law and the prophets.

If only both pseudo-Christians and men of science understood and preached to children and to the uneducated these simple, clear, and necessary truths as they now preach their complicated, confused, and unnecessary theories, all men would uniformly understand the meaning of their lives and recognize one and the same duties as flowing from this meaning.

IX

But "How are we to act now, immediately among ourselves, in Russia, at this moment, when our foes have already attacked us, are killing our people, and threatening us; what should be the action," I shall be asked, "of a Russian soldier, officer, general, Tsar, private individual? Are we, forsooth, to allow our enemies to ruin our possessions, to seize the productions of our labors, to carry away prisoners, or kill our men? What are we to do now that this thing has begun?"

But before the work of war was commenced, by whomsoever it was commenced—every awakened man must answer—before all else the work of my life was commenced. And the work of my life has nothing in common with recognition of the rights of the Chinese, Japanese, or Russians to Port Arthur. The work of my life consists in fulfilling the will of Him who sent me into this life. This will is known to me. This will is that I should love my neighbor and serve him. Then why should I, following temporary, casual, irrational, and cruel demands, deviate from the known eternal and changeless law of all my life? If there be a God, He will not ask me when I die (which may happen at any moment) whether I retained Chi-nam-po with its timber stores, or Port Arthur, or even that conglomeration which is called the Russian Empire, which He did not confide to my care; but He will ask me what I have done with that life which He put at my disposal;—did I use it for the purpose for which it was predestined, and under the conditions for fulfilling which it was intrusted to me? Have I fulfilled His law?

So that to this question as to what is to be done now, when war is commenced, for me, a man who understands his destiny, whatever position I may occupy, there can be no other answer than this, whatever be my circumstances, whether the war be commenced or not, whether thousands of Russians or Japanese be killed, whether not only Port Arthur be taken, but St. Petersburg and Moscow—I cannot act otherwise than as God demands of me, and that therefore I as a man can neither directly nor indirectly, neither by directing, nor by helping, nor by inciting to it, participate in war; I cannot, I do not wish to, and I will not. What will happen immediately or soon, from my ceasing to do that which is contrary to the will of God, I do not and cannot know; but I believe that from the fulfilment of the will of God there can follow nothing but that which is good for me and for all men.

You speak with horror about what might happen if we Russians at this moment ceased to fight, and surrendered to the Japanese what they desire from us. But if it be true that the salvation of mankind from brutalization and self-destruction lies only in the establishment amongst men of that true religion which demands that we should love our neighbor and serve him (with which it is impossible to disagree), then every war, every hour of war, and my participation in it, only renders more difficult and distant the realization of this only possible salvation.

So that, even if one places oneself on the unstable point of view of defining actions according to their presumed consequences—even then the surrender to the Japanese by the Russians of all which the former desire of us, besides the unquestionable advantage of the cessation of ruin and slaughter, would be an approach to the only means of the salvation of mankind from destruction; whereas the continuance of the war, however it may end, will be a postponement of that only means of salvation.

"Yet even if this be so," it is replied, "wars can cease only when all men, or the majority, will refuse to participate in them. But the refusal of one man, whether he be Tsar or soldier, would only, unnecessarily, and without the slightest profit to any one, ruin his life. If the Russian Tsar were now to throw up the war, he would be dethroned, perhaps killed, in order to get rid of him; if an ordinary man were to refuse military service, he would be sent to a penal battalion and perhaps shot. Why, then, without the slightest use should one throw away one's life, which may be profitable to society?" is the common question of those who do not think of the destination of their life and therefore do not understand it.

But this is not what is said and felt by any man who understands the destination of his life—*i.e.* by any religious man. Such a man is guided in his activity not by the presumed consequences of his action, but by the consciousness of the destination of his life. A factory workman goes to his factory and in it accomplishes the work which is allotted him without considering what will be the consequences of his labor. In the same way a soldier acts, carrying out the will of his commanders. So acts a religious man in fulfilling the work prescribed to him by God, without arguing as to what precisely will come of that work. Therefore for a religious man there is no question as to whether many or few men act as he does, or of what may happen to him if he does that which he should do. He knows that besides life and death nothing can happen, and that life and death are in the hands of God whom he obeys.

A religious man acts thus and not otherwise, not because he desires to act thus, nor because it is advantageous to himself or to other men, but because, believing that his life is in the hands of God, he cannot act otherwise.

In this lies the distinction of the activity of religious men; and therefore it is that the salvation of men from the calamities which they inflict upon themselves can be realized only in that degree in which they are guided in their lives, not by advantage nor arguments, but by religious consciousness.

X

"But how about the enemies that attack us?"

"Love your enemies, and ye will have none," is said in the teaching of the Twelve Apostles. This answer is not merely words, as those may imagine who are accustomed to think that the recommendation of love to one's enemies is something hyperbolical, and signifies not that which expressed, but something else. This answer is the indication of a very clear and definite activity, and of its consequences.

To love one's enemies—the Japanese, the Chinese, those yellow people toward whom benighted men are now endeavoring to excite our hatred—to love them means not to kill them for the purpose of having the right of poisoning them with opium, as did the English; not to kill them in order to seize their land, as was done by the French, the Russians, and the Germans; not to bury them alive in punishment for injuring roads, not to tie them together by their hair, not to drown them in their river Amur, as did the Russians.

"A disciple is not above his master.... It is enough for a disciple that he be as his master."

To love the yellow people, whom we call our foes, means, not to teach them under the name of Christianity absurd superstitions about the fall of man, redemption, resurrection, etc., not to teach them the art of deceiving and killing others, but to teach them justice, unselfishness, compassion, love—and that not by words, but by the example of our own good life. And what have we been doing to them, and are still doing?

If we did indeed love our enemies, if even now we began to love our enemies, the Japanese, we would have no enemy.

Therefore, however strange it may appear to those occupied with military plans, preparations, diplomatic considerations, administrative, financial, economical measures, revolutionary, socialistic propaganda, and various unnecessary sciences, by which they think to save mankind from its calamities, the deliverance of man, not only from the calamities of war, but also from all the calamities which men inflict upon themselves, will take place not through emperors or kings instituting peace alliances, not through those who would dethrone emperors, kings, or restrain them by constitutions, or substitute republics for monarchies, not by peace conferences, not by the realization of socialistic programmes, not by victories or defeats on land or sea, not by libraries or universities, nor by those futile mental exercises which are now called science; but only by there being more and more of those simple men who, like the Dukhobors, Drojjin, Olkhovik, in Russia, the Nazarenes in Austria, Condatier in France, Tervey in Holland, and others, having placed as their object not external alterations of life, but the closest fulfilment in themselves of the will of Him who has sent them into life, will direct all their powers to this realization. Only such people realizing the Kingdom of God in themselves, in their souls, will establish, without directly aiming at this purpose, that external Kingdom of God which every human soul is longing for.

Salvation will come to pass only in this one way and not in any other. Therefore what is now being done by those who, ruling men, inspire them with religious and patriotic superstitions, exciting in them exclusiveness, hatred, and murder, as well as by those who, for the purpose of freeing men from slavery and oppression, invoke them to violent external revolution, or think that the acquisition by men of very much incidental and for the most part unnecessary information will of itself bring them to a good life—all this, by distracting men from what alone they need, only removes them further from the possibility of salvation.

The evil from which the men of the Christian world suffer is that they have temporarily lost religion.

Some people, having come to see the discord between the existing religion and the degree of mental and scientific development attained by humanity at the present time, have decided that in general no religion whatever is necessary. They live without religion and preach the uselessness of any religion of whatever kind. Others, holding to that distorted form of the Christian religion which is now preached, likewise live without religion, professing empty external forms, which cannot serve as guidance for men.

Yet a religion which answers to the demands of our time does exist and is known to all men, and in a latent state lives in the hearts of men of the Christian world. Therefore that this religion should become evident to and binding upon all men, it is only necessary that educated men—the leaders of the masses—should understand that religion is necessary to man, that without religion men cannot live a good life, and that what they call science cannot replace religion; and that those in power and who support the old empty forms of religion should understand that what they support and preach under the form of religion is not only not religion, but is the chief obstacle to men's appropriating the true religion which they already know, and which can alone deliver them from their calamities. So that the only certain means of man's salvation consists merely in ceasing to do that which hinders men from assimilating the true religion which already lives in their consciousness.

XI

I had finished this writing when news came of the destruction of six hundred innocent lives opposite Port Arthur. It would seem that the useless suffering and death of these unfortunate deluded men who have needlessly and so dreadfully perished ought to disabuse those who were the cause of this destruction. I am not alluding to Makaroff and other officers—all these men knew what they were doing, and wherefore, and they voluntarily, for personal advantage, for ambition, did as they did, disguising themselves in pretended patriotism, a pretence not condemned merely because it is universal. I allude rather to those unfortunate men drawn from all parts of Russia, who, by the help of religious fraud, and under fear of punishment, have been torn from an honest, reasonable, useful, laborious family life, driven to the other end of the world, placed on a cruel, senseless machine for slaughter, and torn to bits, drowned along with this stupid machine in a distant sea, without any need or any possibility of advantage from all their privations, efforts, and sufferings, or from the death which overtook them.

In 1830, during the Polish war, the adjutant Vilijinsky sent to St. Petersburg by Klopitsky, in a conversation held in French with Dibitch, in answer to the latter's demand that the Russian troops should enter Poland, said to him:—

"Monsieur le Maréchal, I think that in that case it will be quite impossible for the Polish nation to accept this manifesto...."

"Believe me, the Emperor will make no further concessions."

"Then I foresee that, unhappily, there will be war, that much blood will be shed, there will be many unfortunate victims."

"Do not think so; at most there will be ten thousand who will perish on both sides, and that is all,"[1] said Dibitch in his German accent, quite confident that he, together with another man as cruel and foreign to Russian and Polish life as he was himself,—Nicholas I,—had the right to condemn or not to condemn to death ten or a hundred thousand Russians and Poles.

One hardly believes that this could have been, so senseless and dreadful is it,—and yet it was; sixty thousand maintainers of their families lost their lives owing to the will of those men. And now the same thing is taking place.

In order not to let the Japanese into Manchuria, and to expel them from Korea, not ten thousand, but fifty and more thousands will, according to all probability, be necessary. I do not know whether Nicholas II and Kuropatkin say like Dibitch in so many words that not more than fifty thousand lives will be necessary for this on the Russian side alone, only and only that; but they think it—they cannot but think it, because the work they are doing speaks for itself; that ceaseless stream of unfortunate, deluded Russian peasants now being transported by thousands to the Far East—these are those same not more than fifty thousand live Russian men whom Nicholas Romanoff and Alexis Kuropatkin have decided they may get killed, and who will be killed, in support of those stupidities, robberies, and every kind of abomination which were accomplished in China and Korea by immoral ambitious men now sitting peacefully in their palaces and expecting new glory and new advantage and profit from the slaughter of these fifty thousand unfortunate, defrauded Russian workingmen guilty of nothing and gaining nothing by their sufferings and death. For other people's land, to which the Russians have no right, which has been criminally seized from its legitimate owners, and which, in reality, is not even necessary to the Russians—and also for certain

[1] Vilijinsky adds on his own behalf, "The Field-Marshal did not then think that more than sixty thousand Russians alone would perish in this war, not so much from the enemy's fire as from disease—nor that he would himself be amongst their number."

dark dealings by speculators, who in Korea wished to gain money out of other people's forests—many millions of money are spent, *i.e.* a great part of the labor of the whole of the Russian people, while the future generations of this people are bound by debts, its best workmen are withdrawn from labor, and scores of thousands of its sons are mercilessly doomed to death; and the destruction of these unfortunate men is already begun. More than this: the war is being managed by those who have hatched it so badly, so negligently, all is so unexpected, so unprepared, that, as one paper admits, Russia's chief chance of success lies in the fact that it possesses inexhaustible human material. It is upon this that those rely who send to death scores of thousands of Russian men!

It is frankly said that the regrettable reverses of our fleet must be compensated on the land. In plain language this means that if the authorities have badly directed things on sea, and by their negligence have destroyed not only the nation's millions, but thousands of lives, we can make it up by condemning to death on land several more scores of thousands!

When crawling locusts cross rivers, it happens that the lower layers are drowned until from the bodies of the drowned is formed a bridge over which the upper ranks can pass. In the same way are the Russian people being disposed of. Thus the first lower layer is already beginning to drown, indicating the way to other thousands, who will all likewise perish.

And are the originators, directors, and supporters of this dreadful work beginning to understand their sin, their crime? Not in the least. They are quite persuaded that they have fulfilled, and are fulfilling, their duty, and they are proud of their activity. People speak of the loss of the brave Makaroff, who, as all agree, was able to kill men very cleverly; they deplore the loss of a drowned excellent machine of slaughter which had cost so many millions of roubles; they discuss the question of how to find another murderer as capable as the poor benighted Makaroff; they invent new, still more efficacious, tools of slaughter; and all the guilty men engaged in this dreadful work, from the Tsar to the humblest journalist, all with one voice call for new insanities, new cruelties, for the increase of brutality and hatred of one's fellow-men.

"Makaroff is not the only man in Russia, and every admiral placed in his position will follow in his steps and will continue the plan and the idea of Makaroff, who has nobly perished in the strife," writes the *Novoe Vremya*.

"Let us earnestly pray God for those who have laid down their lives for the sacred Fatherland, without doubting for one moment that the Fatherland will give us new sons, equally virtuous, for the further struggle, and will find in them an inexhaustible store of strength for a worthy completion of the work," writes the St. Petersburg *Viedomosti*.

"A ripe nation will draw no other conclusion from the defeat, however unprecedented, than that we should continue, develop, and conclude the strife; therefore let us find in ourselves new strength; new heroes of the spirit will arise," writes the *Russ*,—and so forth.

So murder and every kind of crime go on with greater fury. People enthusiastically admire the martial spirit of the volunteers who, having come unexpectedly upon fifty of their fellow-men, slay all of them, or take possession of a village and slaughter all its population, or hang or shoot those accused of being spies—*i.e.* of doing the very same thing which is regarded as indispensable and is constantly done on our side. News about these crimes is reported in pompous telegrams to their chief director, the Tsar, who, in return, sends to his virtuous troops his blessing on the continuation of such deeds.

Is it not evident that, if there be a salvation from this position, it is only one: that one which Jesus teaches?—"Seek ye first the Kingdom of God and His righteousness (that which is within you), and all the rest—*i.e.* all that practical welfare toward which man is striving—will of itself be realized."

Such is the law of life: practical welfare is attained not when man strives toward this practical welfare—such striving, on the contrary, for the most part removes man from the attainment of what he seeks; but only when man, without thinking of the attainment of practical welfare, strives toward the most perfect fulfilment of that which before God, before the Source and Law of his life, he regards as right. Then only, incidentally, is practical welfare also attained.

So that the true salvation of men is only one thing: the fulfilment of the will of God by each individual man within himself—*i.e.* in that portion of the universe which alone is subject to his power. In this is the chief, the only, destiny and duty of every individual man, and at the same time this is the only means by which every individual man can influence others; and, therefore, to this, and to this only, should all the efforts of every man be directed.

May 2, 1904.

XII

I had only just despatched the last of the preceding pages of this paper when the dreadful news came of a new iniquity committed in regard to the Russian people by those light-minded men who, crazed with power, have appropriated the right of managing them. Again coarse and servile slaves of slaves, dressed up in various dazzling attires—varieties of Generals wishing to distinguish themselves, or to earn the right to add one more little star, fingle fangle, or scrap of ribbon to their idiotic glaring get-up, or else from stupidity or carelessness—again these miserable men have destroyed amid dreadful sufferings thousands of those honorable, kind, hard-working laborers who feed them. And again this iniquity not only does not cause those responsible for it to reflect and repent, but one hears and reads only about its being necessary as speedily as possible to mutilate and slaughter a greater number of men, and to ruin still more families, both Russian and Japanese.

More than this, to prepare men for fresh iniquities of this kind, the perpetrators of these crimes, far from recognizing what is evident to all—viz. that for the Russians this event, even from their patriotic, military point of view, was a scandalous defeat—endeavor to assure credulous people that these unfortunate Russian laboring men—lured into a trap like cattle into a slaughterhouse, of whom several thousands have been killed and maimed merely because one General did not understand what another General had said—have performed an act of heroism because those who could not run away were killed and those who did run away remained alive. As to the fact that one of these immoral and cruel men, distinguished by the titles of Generals, Admirals, drowned a quantity of peaceful Japanese, this is also described as a great and glorious act of heroism, which must gladden the hearts of Russians. And in all the papers are reprinted this awful appeal to murder:—

"Let the two thousand Russian soldiers killed on the Yalu, together with the maimed *Retvisan* and her sister ships, with our lost torpedo-boats, teach our cruisers with what devastation they must break in upon the shores of base Japan. She has sent her soldiers to shed Russian blood, and no quarter should be afforded her. Now one cannot—it is sinful—be sentimental; we must fight; we must direct such heavy blows that the memory of them shall freeze the treacherous hearts of the Japanese. Now is the time for the cruisers to go out to sea to reduce to ashes the towns of Japan, flying as a dreadful calamity along its shores. No more sentimentality."

The frightful work commenced is continued. Loot, violence, murder, hypocrisy, theft, and, above all, the most fearful fraud—the distortion of religious teachings, both Christian and Buddhistic—continue. The Tsar, the chief responsible person, continues to review the troops, to thank, reward, and encourage them; he issues an edict for the calling out of the reserves; his faithful subjects again and again lay down their property and lives at the feet of him they call, only with their lips, their adored Monarch. On the other hand, desiring to distinguish themselves before each other in deeds and not in words only, they tear away the fathers and the bread-winners from their orphaned families, preparing them for slaughter. The worse the position of Russia, the more recklessly do the journalists lie, transforming shameful defeats into victories, knowing that no one will contradict them; and they quietly collect money from subscriptions and sales. The more money and labor of the people is devoted to the war, the more is grabbed by various authorities and speculators, who know that no one will convict them because every one is doing the same. The military, trained for murder, having passed years in a school of inhumanity, coarseness, and idleness, rejoice—poor men—because, besides an increase of their salary, the slaughter of superiors opens vacancies for their promotion. Christian pastors continue to invite men to the greatest of crimes, continue to commit sacrilege, praying God to help the work of war; and, instead of condemning, they justify and praise that pastor who, with the cross in his hands on the very scene of murder, encouraged men to the crime. The same thing is going on in Japan. The benighted Japanese go in for murder with yet greater fervor, owing to their victories; the Mikado also reviews and rewards his troops; various Generals boast of their bravery, imagining that, having learned to kill, they have acquired enlightenment. So, too, groan the unfortunate working people torn from useful labor and from their families. So their journalists also lie and rejoice over their gains. Also probably—for where murder is elevated into virtue every kind of vice is bound to flourish—also probably all kinds of commanders and speculators earn money; and Japanese theologians and religious teachers no less than the masters in the techniques of armament do not remain behind the Europeans in the techniques of religious deceit and sacrilege, but distort the great Buddhistic teaching by not only permitting but justifying that murder which Buddha forbade. The Buddhistic scientist, Soyen-Shaku, ruling over eight hundred monasteries, explains that although Buddha forbade manslaughter he also said he could never be at peace until all beings are united in the infinitely loving heart of all things, and that, therefore, in order to bring into harmony that which is discordant it is necessary to fight and to kill men.[2]

---

[2] In the article it is said: "This triple world is my own possession. All the things therein are my own children ... the ten thousand things in this world are no more than the reflections of my own self. They come from the one source. They partake of the one body. Therefore I cannot rest, until every being, even the smallest possible fragment of existence, is settled down to its proper appointment.... This is the position taken by the Buddha, and we, his humble followers, are but to walk in his wake. Why, then, do we fight at all? Because we do not find this world as it ought to be. Because there are here so many perverted creatures, so many wayward thoughts, so many ill-directed hearts, due to ignorant subjectivity. For this reason Buddhists are never tired of combating

It is as if there never had existed the Christian and Buddhistic teaching about the unity of the human spirit, the brotherhood of men, love, compassion, the sacredness of human life. Men, both Japanese and Russians, already enlightened by the truth, yet like wild animals, nay, worse than wild animals, throw themselves upon each other with the sole desire to destroy as many lives as possible. Thousands of unfortunates groan and writhe in cruel sufferings and die in agony in Japanese and Russian field hospitals, asking themselves in bewilderment why this fearful thing was done with them, while other thousands are already rotting in the earth or on the earth, or floating in the sea, in swollen decomposition. And scores of thousands of wives, fathers, mothers, children, are bemoaning their bread-winners; uselessly destroyed. Yet all this is still too little; new and newer victims are being prepared. The chief concern of the Russian organizers of slaughter is that on the Russian side the stream of food for cannon—three thousand men per day doomed to destruction—should not be interrupted for one minute. The Japanese are preoccupied with the same thing. The locusts are incessantly being driven down into the river in order that the rows behind may pass over the bodies.

When will this cease, and the deceived people at last recover themselves and say: "Well, go you yourselves, you heartless Tsars, Mikados, Ministers, Bishops, priests, generals, editors, speculators,

---

all productions of ignorance, and their fight must be to the bitter end. They will show no quarter. They will mercilessly destroy the very root from which arises the misery of this life. To accomplish this end, they will never be afraid of sacrificing their lives...." There follow, just as is usual with us, entangled arguments about self-sacrifice and kindness, about the transmigration of souls and about much else—all this for the sole purpose of concealing the simple and clear commandment of Buddha: not to kill. Further it is said: "The hand that is raised to strike and the eye that is fixed to take aim do not belong to the individual, but are the instruments utilized by a principle higher than transient existence." ("The Open Court," May, 1904. "Buddhist Views of War," by the Right Rev. Soyen-Shaku.)

or however you may be called, go you yourselves under these shells and bullets, but we do not wish to go and we will not go. Leave us in peace, to plough, and sow, and build,—and also to feed you." It would be so natural to say this now, when amongst us in Russia resounds the weeping and wailing of hundreds of thousands of mothers, wives, and children, from whom are being snatched away their bread-earners, the so-called "reserve." These same men, the majority of the reserve, are able to read; they know what the Far East is; they know that war is going on, not for anything which is in the least necessary to Russia, but for some dealings in strange land, leased lands, as they themselves call them, on which it seemed advantageous to some corrupt speculators to build railways and so gain profit; also they know, or might know, that they will be killed like sheep in a slaughterhouse, since the Japanese possess the latest improvements in tools of murder, which we do not, as the Russian authorities who are sending these people to death had not thought in time of furnishing themselves with the same weapons as the Japanese. Knowing all this, it would indeed be so natural to say, "Go you, those who have brought on this work, all you to whom war is necessary, and who justify it; go you, and face the Japanese bullets and mines, but we will not go, because we not only do not need to do this, but we cannot understand how it can be necessary to any one."

But no, they do not say this; they go, and they will continue to go; they cannot but go as long as they fear that which ruins the body and not that which ruins both the body and the soul. "Whether we shall be killed," they argue, "or maimed in these chinnampos, or whatever they are called, whither we are driven, we do not know; it yet may happen that we shall get through safely, and, moreover, with rewards and glory, like those sailors who are now being feasted all over Russia because the Japanese bombs and bullets did not hit them, but somebody else; whereas should we refuse, we should be certainly sent to prison, starved, beaten, exiled to the province of Yakoutsk, perhaps even killed immediately." So with despair in their hearts, leaving behind a good rational life, leaving their wives and their children,—they go.

Yesterday I met a Reservist soldier accompanied by his mother and wife. All three were riding in a cart; he had had a drop too much; his wife's face was swollen with tears. He turned to me:—

"Good-by to thee! Lyof Nikolaevitch, off to the Far East."

"Well, art thou going to fight?"

"Well, some one has to fight!"

"No one need fight!"

He reflected for a moment. "But what is one to do; where can one escape?"

I saw that he had understood me, had understood that the work to which he was being sent was an evil work.

"Where can one escape?" That is the precise expression of that mental condition which in the official and journalistic world is translated into the words—"For the Faith, the Tsar, and the Fatherland." Those who, abandoning their hungry families, go to suffering, to death, say as they feel, "Where can one escape?" Whereas those who sit in safety in their luxurious palaces say that all Russian men are ready to sacrifice their lives for their adored Monarch, and for the glory and greatness of Russia.

Yesterday, from a peasant I know, I received two letters, one after the other. This is the first:—

"Dear Lyof Nikolaevitch,—Well, to-day I have received the official announcement of my call to the Service; to-morrow I must present myself at the headquarters. That is all. And after that—to the Far East to meet the Japanese bullets. About my own and my household's grief I will not tell you; it is not you who will fail to understand all the horror of my position and the horrors of war; all this you have long ago painfully realized, and you understand it all. How I have longed to visit you, to have a talk with you! I had written to you a long letter in which I described the torments of my soul; but I had not had time to copy it, when I received my summons. What is my wife to do now with her four children? As an old man, of course, you cannot do anything yourself for my folks, but you might ask some of your friends in their leisure to visit my orphaned family. I beg you earnestly that if my wife proves unable to bear the agony of her helplessness with her burden of children and makes up her mind to go to you for help and counsel, you will receive and console her. Although she does not know you personally, she believes in your word, and that means much. I was not able to resist the summons, but I say beforehand that through me not one Japanese family shall be orphaned. My God! how dreadful is all this—how distressing and painful to abandon all by which one lives and in which one is concerned."

The second letter is as follows: "Kindest Lyof Nikolaevitch, Only one day of actual service has passed, and I have already lived through an eternity of most desperate torments. From 8 o'clock in the morning till 9 in the evening we have been crowded and knocked about to and fro in the barrack yard, like a herd of cattle. The comedy of medical examination was three times repeated, and those who had reported themselves ill did not receive even ten minutes' attention before they were marked 'Satisfactory.' When we, these two thousand satisfactory individuals, were driven from the military commander to the barracks, along the road spread out for almost a verst stood a crowd of relatives, mothers, and wives with infants in arms; and if you had only heard and seen how they clasped their fathers, husbands, sons, and hanging round their necks wailed hopelessly! Generally I behave in a reserved way and can restrain my feelings, but I could not hold out, and I also wept. [In journalistic language this same is expressed thus: "The upheaval of patriotic feeling is immense."] Where is the standard that can measure all this immensity of woe now spreading itself over almost one-third of the world? And we, we are now that food for cannon, which in the near future will be offered as sacrifice to the God of vengeance and horror. I cannot manage to establish my inner balance. Oh! how I execrate myself for this double-mindedness which prevents my serving one Master and God."

This man does not yet sufficiently believe that what destroys the body is not dreadful, but that which destroys both the body and the soul, therefore he cannot refuse to go; yet while leaving his own family he promises beforehand that through him not one Japanese family shall be orphaned; he believes in the chief law of God, the law of all religions—to act toward others as one wishes others to act toward oneself. Of such men more or less consciously recognizing this law, there are in our time, not in the Christian world alone, but in the Buddhistic, Mahomedan, Confucian, and Brahminic world, not only thousands but millions.

There exist true heroes, not those who are now being fêted because, having wished to kill others, they were not killed themselves, but true heroes, who are now confined in prisons and in the province of Yakoutsk for having categorically refused to enter the ranks of murderers, and who have preferred martyrdom to this departure from the law of Jesus. There are also such as he who writes to me, who go, but who will not kill. But also that majority which goes without thinking, and endeavors not to think of what it is doing, still in the depth of its soul does now already feel that it is doing an evil deed by obeying authorities who tear men from labor and from their families and send them to needless slaughter of men, repugnant to their soul and their faith; and they go only because they are so entangled on all sides that—"Where can one escape?"

Meanwhile those who remain at home not only feel this, but know and express it. Yesterday in the high road I met some peasants returning from Toula. One of them was reading a leaflet as he walked by the side of his cart.

I asked, "What is that—a telegram?"

"This is yesterday's,—but here is one of to-day." He took another out of his pocket. We stopped. I read it.

"You should have seen what took place yesterday at the station," he said; "it was dreadful. Wives, children, more than a thousand of them, weeping. They surrounded the train, but were allowed no further. Strangers wept, looking on. One woman from Toula gasped and fell down dead. Five children. They have since been placed in various institutions; but the father was driven away all the same.... What do we want with this Manchuria, or whatever it is called? There is sufficient land here. And what a lot of people and of property has been destroyed."

Yes, the relation of men to war is now quite different from that which formerly existed, even so lately as the year '77. That which is now taking place never took place before.

The papers set forth that, during the receptions of the Tsar, who is travelling about Russia for the purpose of hypnotizing the men who are being sent to murder, indescribable enthusiasm is manifested amongst the people. As a matter of fact, something quite different is being manifested. From all sides one hears reports that in one place three Reservists have hanged themselves; in another spot, two more; in yet another, about a woman whose husband had been taken away bringing her children to the conscription committee-room and leaving them there; while another hanged herself in the yard of the military commander. All are dissatisfied, gloomy, exasperated. The words, "For the Faith, the King, and the Fatherland," the National Anthem, and shouts of "Hurrah" no longer act upon people as they once did. Another warfare of a different kind—the struggling consciousness of the deceit and sinfulness of the work to which people are being called—is more and more taking possession of the people.

Yes, the great strife of our time is not that now taking place between the Japanese and the Russians, nor that which may blaze up between the white and yellow races, not that strife which is carried on by mines, bombs, bullets, but that spiritual strife which without ceasing has gone on and is now going on between the enlightened consciousness of mankind now waiting for manifestation and that darkness and that burden which surrounds and oppresses mankind.

In His own time Jesus yearned in expectation, and said, "I came to cast fire upon the earth, and how I wish that it were already kindled." Luke xii. 49.

That which Jesus longed for is being accomplished, the fire is being kindled. Then do not let us check it, but let us spread and serve it.

13 May, 1904.

I should never finish this paper if I were to continue to add to it all that corroborates its essential idea. Yesterday the news came in of the sinking of the Japanese ironclads; and in the so-called higher circles of Russian fashionable, rich, intellectual society they are, without the slightest conscientious scruples, rejoicing at the destruction of a thousand human lives. Yet to-day I have received from a simple seaman, a man standing on the lowest plane of society, the following letter:[3]

"Much respected Lyof Nikolaevitch, I greet you with a low bow, with love, much respected Lyof Nikolaevitch. I have read your book. It was very pleasant reading for me. I have been a great lover of reading your works. Well, Lyof Nikolaevitch, we are now in a state of war, please write to me whether it is agreeable to God or not that our commanders compel us to kill. I beg you, Lyof Nikolaevitch, write to me please whether or not the truth now exists on earth. Tell me, Lyof Nikolaevitch. In church here a prayer is being read, the priest mentions the Christ-loving army. Is it true or not that God loves war? I pray you, Lyof Nikolaevitch, have you got any books from which I could see whether truth exists on earth or not? Send me such books. What they cost, I will pay. I beg you, Lyof Nikolaevitch, do not neglect my request. If there are no books then send me a letter. I will be very glad when I receive a letter from you. I will await your letter with impatience. Good-by for the present. I remain alive and well and wish the same to you from the Lord God. Good health and good success in your work."

THE END

[3] The letter is written in a most illiterate way, filled with mistakes in orthography and punctuation.

www.ingramcontent.com/pod-product-compliance
Ingram Content Group UK Ltd.
Pitfield, Milton Keynes, MK11 3LW, UK
UKHW040317300826
14791UKWH00003B/954

9 789354 629747